EARTH, SEA, SKY

EARTH, SEA, SKY

IMAGES AND MĀORI PROVERBS FROM THE
NATURAL WORLD OF AOTEAROA NEW ZEALAND

CRAIG
POTTON
PUBLISHING

HUIA PUBLISHERS

First published in 2003, reprinted in 2004
by Huia Publishers,
39 Pipitea Street, PO Box 17-335,
Wellington, Aotearoa New Zealand
www.huia.co.nz
and
Craig Potton Publishing
98 Vickerman Street, Nelson,
Aotearoa New Zealand
www.craigpotton.co.nz

ISBN 1-877283-99-1
Text © 2003 Patricia and Waiariki Grace

Photographs © 2003 Craig Potton

National Library of New Zealand Cataloguing-in-Publication Data
Grace, Patricia, 1937-
Earth, sea, sky : images and Māori proverbs from the natural
world of Aotearoa New Zealand / by Patricia and Waiariki Grace ;
photographs by Craig Potton.
ISBN 1-877283-99-1
1. Proverbs, Maori. 2. New Zealand-Pictorial works. I. Grace,
Waiariki. II. Potton, Craig. III Title.
398.999442-dc 21

Published with the assistance of

Te Waka Toi

Whakataka te hau ki te uru

Whakataka te hau ki te tonga

Kia mākinakina i uta

Kia mātaratara i tai

Kia hī ake ana te atakura

He tio, he huka, he hauhunga

Tīhei mauri ora!

Let the cold winds from the west

and from the south, that assail

the lands and seas, desist.

Let the red-tipped dawn come

with a touch of frost, a sharpened

air, the promise of a glorious day.

Behold, we live!

Greetings and introduction

E ngā mana, e ngā reo, e ngā karangatanga maha huri āwhiotia i ngā tōpito o te aotūroa, tēnā koutou katoa.

Tēnā koutou i runga i ngā āhuatanga maha e uruhia mai nei i a tātou katoa, ahakoa ko wai, ahakoa nō hea.

Tēnei te mihi whānui atu ki te hunga kua riro ki te kāpunipunitanga o ngā wairua. Kua mihia, kua tangihia rātou, nō reira ko te whakatau noa ake, ko rātou ki a rātou, ko tātou ki a tātou. Nō reira, kia ora huihui mai tātou katoa.

Greetings to you all, the peoples of the four winds, the chiefly descendants of the spiritual homelands. We welcome you warmly and remember with love those who have passed on to spiritual realms. We think ahead to those not yet born who will one day be welcomed as part of our families.

People of every nation have their own wisdoms, teachings and inspirational utterings which have existed since before the time of literacy. The messages contained in the following pages have been compiled mostly from traditional sources – ancient proverbs, songs and chants.

In the Māori tradition people are part of the universe, there being an interdependence among all life forms and all aspects of the physical and spiritual worlds. It is through care of, and respect for, the lands, waters and atmosphere that our physical and spiritual sustenance and survival is assured. Therefore there is a need to live in harmony with nature rather than attempt to conquer and rule it.

This publication offers some Māori perspectives of our home environment in Aotearoa New Zealand, and invites you to unite with us in acknowledging the spiritual power and essence of nature which sustains us all.

Korihi ake ngā manu
Tākiri mai te ata
Ka ao, ka ao, ka awatea!
Tīhei mauri ora.

The birds call
The day begins
And I am alive.

With the dawn comes a sense of well-being and optimism. (Trad.)

Rārangi maunga, tū tonu, tū tonu.

Rārangi tangata, ngaro noa, ngaro noa.

You have gone

But your mountain

Is everlasting.

Though people die, mountains remain and all is not lost. (Trad.)

Rere atu, rere mai

Taku manu e

Rere ki tua, rere ki kō

Kia whetūrangitia e.

Fly, my bird

in every direction.

Attain

the countless stars.

Contemporary poetry.

Hutia te rito o te pū harakeke

Kei whea te kōmako e kō?

From where

Will the bellbird sing?

A plea for conservation. If you destroy the flax plant, from where will the bellbird sing? (Trad.)

Hineruhe, te wahine nāna i tū te ata hāpara.

It is Hineruhe, maker of dawn.

A new dawn is symbolic of renewed opportunities. (Trad.)

Rimu rimu

Rere ana

Korowai aroha e.

Wrap me again

In bright weed

Which will be

A blanket for me.

When the tide ebbs, seaweed seems to flow away from the land. Here this is likened
to the departure of loved ones to the spiritual world. (Contemporary poetry.)

Ko te rā māeneene

Ā te rāhui Tangaroa.

On a calm, warm day

Tangaroa rests.

Tangaroa is the sea god. No matter what turmoil life may hold,
there are always periods of calm.

Matariki ahunga nui
Matariki tāpuapua
Matariki hunga nui
Ngā kai a Matariki
Nāna i ao ake ki runga.

When Pleiades,
the gatherer,
is bright in the sky
the year begins.

The Māori year begins in winter. This beginning is signalled by the rising of Matariki, the
Pleiades. Crops have been harvested and the ground prepares itself for spring. (Trad.)

E huri tō aroaro ki Parawera-nui,
ki Tahu-makaka-nui.

Ice-cold winds,
Sleet-filled winds,
Rolling cloud and
Thunder.

Face up to adversity. Don't walk away. (Trad.)

Takoto kau ana te whānau a Tāne.

The descendants of Tāne
Are laid low.

Tāne is the god of forests. This is a plea for conservation.

He kākano i ruia mai i Rangiatea.

The seed will not be lost.

This proverb asserts resilience. Rangiatea is the spiritual homeland of the Māori people.
Although much may be lost, the Māori people, seeds of Rangiatea, will remain. (Trad.)

Kia whakapapa pounamu

te moana

kia teretere

te kārohirohi e.

May the days ignite –

as sunlight

on greenstone waters.

Greenstone, or pounamu, is New Zealand jade. Here it is used descriptively for shining seas, which in turn express a wish for bright futures. (Trad.)

Kei te haereere a Hine-pūkohu-rangi,
me tona kete whaowhao rangi.

Hine-pūkohu-rangi,
mist-maker,
empties her baskets
across the sky.

Mist descending is a portent of something momentous or calamitous. (Trad.)

Hupane, kaupane
Whiti te rā.

A new sunrise,
A new day.

Fighting chief Te Rauparaha was hiding in a covered pit. As his enemy approached
he mused on his fate. Would it be life, or would it be death? His enemy passed by.
He ascended into daylight, and life. One can emerge from difficult situations to
seek new opportunities. (Trad.)

Kimihia te kahurangi;

ki te piko tōu matenga, ki te maunga teitei.

If you bow your head

let it be only

to a great mountain.

Know one's own worth and capabilities. Persevere. (Trad.)

Hinga atu he tētē kura,
ara mai he tētē kura.

One fern frond falls
as another unfurls.

As one leader dies there will always be another to take their place. (Trad.)

Ngā uaua o Papatūānuku.

By the forest vines
Earth and Sky
were bound together.

In the Māori creation story, before the time of light, the primal parents Earth and Sky lay together
in darkness, bound by vines. They were thrust apart, light came to the earth and life as we know
it evolved. (Trad.)

He toka tū moana, arā he toa rongonui.

Your strength is like a rock that
stands in raging waters.

Affirming an individual's strength and courage. (Trad.)

He taru kahika.

Walk on,
as it is only summer rain falling.

It is only a small adversity, so don't let it be a hindrance. (Trad.)

He tau kotipū.

A year cut short
is a year of early winter.

An unexpected frost, heralding an early winter, upsets the yearly cycle of life. Unexpected adversity is more difficult to deal with than adversity known in advance. (Trad.)

I hea koe i te ao o te kōwhai?

Where were you

when the kōwhai was in bud?

The abundant yellow flowers of the kōwhai tree are a sign of spring. This is a question for those who failed to plant in springtime, or who were not present when there was work to be done, yet still wish to reap the benefits. (Trad.)

Te ara kura o Tāne.

Glittering pathway of the
setting sun.

A potential leader sets out on a pathway to success. (Trad.)

Te tāpaepae o te rangi.

See there, to the place
where the sky reaches down.

Strive to attain the utmost. Look to the furthest horizon. (Trad.)

Māra kūmara a Ngatoro-i-rangi.

A sky as speckled as
the kūmara plantation
of Ngatoro-i-rangi.

A person of various skills is compared to Ngatoro-i-rangi, a great leader whose
talents were manifold. (Trad.)

Piki atu au ki te taumata o tōku maunga,

Ka kite au i te mana, i te ihi o te whenua nei nō ōku tīpuna.

I climb to the summit
of my mountain
to see the lands
of my ancestors.

People return to the lands of their ancestors to reconnect with their roots and customs. (Trad.)

He iti hau marangai e tū te pāhokahoka.

First comes the light wind, carrying rain,
then comes the rainbow.

Be positive, look on the bright side. (Trad.)

He ua ki te pō, he paewai ki te ao.

When it rains at night, eels may be caught in the morning.

A figurative expression which implies that rain will disguise preparations for attacking one's enemy. (Trad.)

Nā Tāne i toko, ka mawehe a Rangi rāua ko Papa,

nāna i tauwehea ai, ka heuea te Pō, ka heuea te Ao.

It is by the strength of Tāne

that Sky and Earth

were separated

and Light was born.

In the Māori creation story it was Tāne, god of forests, who separated Earth and Sky,
allowing light to shine on the earth, so freeing the world from darkness. This is often used as
a metaphor for the attainment of knowledge or enlightenment. (Trad.)

Tangi ana ngā tai
Rū ana te whenua.

Listen to the roar of the sea
Feel the land tremble.

The anger and intense feelings of the Māori people cannot be ignored when
it comes to their being dispossesed of land. (Trad.)

Ka whaimata te tapuae o Tangaroa.

Tangaroa. Ka haruru.

He strides to and fro, Tangaroa.

Hear him roar.

Tangaroa is the god of the sea. Unwelcome events create a strong reaction. (Trad.)

Ko Poutū-te-rangi te mātahi o te tau.

It is Poutū-te-rangi,
the month of March,
bringing her first fruits.

Autumn is harvest time, the time when the results of one's endeavours begin to show. (Trad.)

Te anu o Takurua.

It is Sirius
wearing his winter cloak.

Life changes are as inevitable as seasonal changes. Takurua is also known as Sirius, sometimes called the Dog Star. It is prominent in the Southern Hemisphere in winter. (Trad.)

Titiro kau ana ko ngā pari pōhatu

E whakaatu atu nei i ngā tīpuna.

I look to the rock cliffs

and see the faces

of my ancestors.

People belong to the land and care for it from generation to generation. (Trad.)

Ka parangia nei te aotūroa
i te pō kerekere.

Intense night envelops
the world.

Darkness is a metaphor for ignorance and intolerance. (Trad.)

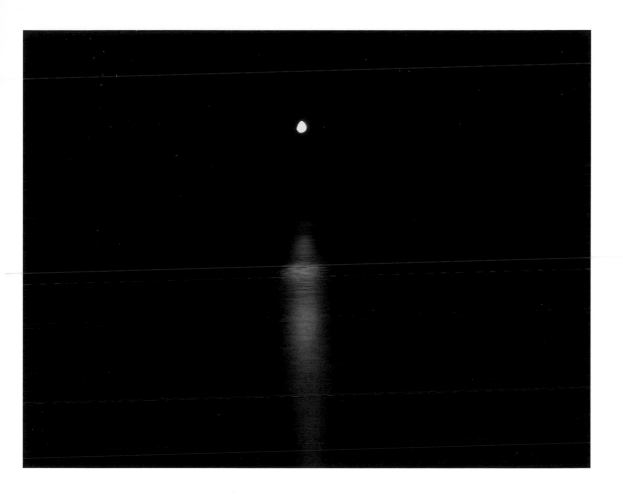

Tirohia ki a Aorangi
Ka kākahutia e te huka rere.

Look at Aorangi
clothed in snow.

Aorangi is New Zealand's highest mountain. Look to those who have achieved greatness, and know it took a lifetime. (Trad.)

He manga wai koia
kia kore e whitikia.

It is a big river indeed that
cannot be crossed.

Given time and effort most things are achievable, but let us always understand
our human limitations. (Trad.)

Tangi kau ana te hau
ki runga o marae nui
o Hinemoana.

The wind sails across
the vast ocean plaza of Hinemoana.

Hinemoana is the ocean spirit. A message of sorrow is carried by the wind to all places. (Trad.)

E hī ake ana te atakura.

He tio, he huka, he hauhunga.

The red dawn comes

with a sharpened air,

a touch of frost,

the promise of a glorious day.

A wish that challenges will be met and that futures will be bright. (Trad.)

Waikato taniwha rau,

he piko he taniwha,

he piko he taniwha.

Waikato,

home of many chiefs.

There is a taniwha (a monstrous water creature) at every bend of the Waikato River, the North Island's longest river. By metaphorically calling a chief a taniwha this saying evokes the fearsome sublimity of the chiefs who live along the river's length. (Trad.)

Te ara o tukutuku
pūngawerewere.

The pathway of the spider.

Said in praise of something intricate and beautiful. (Trad.)

Tuia te rangi e tū iho nei

Tuia te papa e takoto nei.

Join sky above

to earth below,

just as people join together.

As sky joins to earth, so people join together. People depend on one another. (Trad.)

Ka piki e te tai,
piki tū piki rere.

The tide rises
In and out it flows.

People come and go. Life goes on. (Trad.)

Tīhore ana te rangi

i te uira.

Lightning splits the heavens.

Life has its dramatic phases. (Trad.)

E tō, e te rā,

rehurehu ki te rua.

Sun above,

descend into the abyss.

This is a metaphor regarding the inevitability of death. (Trad.)

Captions